A FAMILY SECRET

Drawings
Eric Heuvel
Scenario
Eric Heuvel
Menno Metselaar
Ruud van der Rol
Hans Groeneweg
Translation
Lorraine T. Miller

© 2005
Eric Heuvel
Zaandam

· ERIC HEUVEL ·

A FAMILY SECRET

Anne Frank House / Resistance Museum Friesland

Jeroen only has a few days left to gather up some old things for the Queen's Day flea market.

Maybe, I should have called first.

There's gotta be great stuff at Gran's!

Jeroen, sweet boy! Here to see your old granny again?

Yes, Grandma... but I also need a favor...

So you want to poke around in my attic for things to sell at the flea market?

Please!

Hmm... all right, but let's have a cup of tea first.

I've already found lots of old things in our attic, but I bet there's something here as well.

Show me what you plan to take with you, okay?

Is there lots of stuff in the attic?

Yes, your grandpa saved everything... I haven't been in the attic for years...

What a mess!

5

Thanks a lot, Grandpa! Now where to begin?

Years of monthly magazines about sport fishing. Well, not exactly a hot item!

What a beautiful dagger! I wonder where it's from?!

What's in this closet, let's see... AAAAAHHH !!!

ARE YOU OKAY, JEROEN?

Fine Gran... an old owl here just gave me a scare!

Nice hat, wonder what can I get for it?

Lots of stuff, but nothing worth much!

More junk that nobody really needs.

Huh, what's this?!?

6

A cloth star... Jew? Strange...

The 1936 Olympic Games in Berlin! Wow, that was a long time ago!

3 gold medals! Why wouldn't Hitler shake his hand?

JESSE OWENS WINT 3ᵉ GOUD

HITLER WEIGE ZWARTE ATLEE TE FELICITERE

I wonder who made this?

DUITSCHE JEUGD IN DEN HITLER-JUGEND

JOODSCHE VL WIJKEN UIT N

DUITSCH LEGER STEEDS STERKER

Jeroen is not aware of how much time has passed...

Clippings from before WWII...

wie volgt?
HITLER IN PRAAG!
Rusland v... Finland binnen
VREDE IN ONZE TIJD!
Duitschland één grote kazerne
Vervolging Joden in Duitschland verscherpt
Burgeroorlog in Spanje
Japan neemt Nanking in
Akkoord te München
Crisis om Sudetenland

Maybe there's a name somewhere...

Helena? That's Gran! So this belongs to her...

Helena & Esther 1939

Jeroen! You still alive? You're awfully quiet!

Uh,... yeah... Everything's fine. Hey Grandma! I found your scrapbook!

Isn't this yours?

Grandma, aren't you happy that I found it?

Oh, dear... it was so long ago...

I'll tell you why I started this album.

Okay...

Let's hope this doesn't take too long!

It's very hard to talk about what happened... Such a dreadful time, so we never discussed it in our family... It's a family secret...

I was 12 when I started this scrapbook. That was in 1938. I kept track of the news. My older brothers thought I was a bookworm. They were always fighting with each other.

The German Chancellor, Hitler, is being welcomed by an enthusiastic crowd.

You're a cheater!

I don't wanna play anymore!

Theo, Wim, stop arguing!

A person can't even hear the news.

My father was a policeman and we lived in Amsterdam.

What's for dinner? I'm starved!

Meatloaf, boiled potatoes...

So, you're the one with blond hair, but who's this pretty girl?

Helena & Esther 1939

Sigh... Esther...

Esther was my best friend. She was originally from Germany...

It's as if it were yesterday... Esther coming to live next door. Yet, it was the winter of 1938.

Our downstairs neighbors had already heard who was going to live in the empty apartment...

It seems they're Jews from Germany...

How can that be...I thought they closed the Dutch borders to refugees in May?

I was very curious about our new neighbors...

Do you see a moving truck?

No, just a car...

Actually, the people in that car were our new neighbors.

Your new home is there on the third floor...

The apartment is a bit small, but with such short notice, it was difficult to find anything else, Dr. Hecht...

...it will do just fine...

Hi there, I'm Helena!

Ich heiße Esther...

I was glad Esther was placed in my class at school.

Boys and girls, this is Esther. She's from Karlsruhe in Germany. Do your best to make her feel at home.

tien daagse veldtocht → 18:

1870 Franse oor

We worked on Esther's Dutch everyday on our way home from school.

When you can pronounce the city of "Scheveningen" in Dutch, then you've got it...

Shev, Schefe...ening..eh

Not everyone was happy with the new neighbors.

What are all these foreigners doing here?

So many people are already out of work!

In no time, Esther could speak Dutch. She began to tell me stories about Germany... dreadful stories.

We had to flee... I had to leave all my stuff behind in Germany. I could only take some clothes...

Was it that bad?

Yes, it all started in 1933, when Hitler's party came to power.

Once we get rid of Germany's Jews, there'll be no more poverty and unemployment!

Heil Hitler! All right!

One of the first things Hitler did was to abolish other political parties. He was a dictator from then on.

If you're not with us, you're against us! And you'll feel our wrath!

Hitler had gangs of thugs... the S.A.* Lots of his opponents were beaten-up and many were imprisoned in concentration camps.

Now we're in charge!

I'll teach you, you filthy socialist!

From now on, might is right!

* Storm Troopers

There was some resistance, but this was dangerous. Our neighbor was arrested... a very nice man.

They're taking him to a concentration camp!

Shhh...

What an outrage!

He should have just kept his mouth shut!

Jews were also dealt with. My father is a doctor, but all of a sudden he was only allowed to treat Jewish patients. The Nazis hung a sign on his office door as a warning to non-Jews.

Nobody will dare visit this Jew doctor now!

Good, he'll go bankrupt!

Dr. med. M. Hecht
Achtung Jude!
Besuch verboten

I'm still not changing doctors!

More and more Germans supported Hitler. Unemployment and poverty had decreased because Hitler was building a powerful army.

Germany isn't big enough for us. We must have more land!

I will make Germany a mighty nation again!

New factories and highways were constructed...

A new and prosperous Germany...

These new roads are going to come in handy!

Reichs-autobahn Nürnberg München

Teachers who disagreed with the Nazis were fired. Children were taught to hate the Jews.

I repeat the words of our leader Adolf Hitler: The Jew is our greatest enemy.

"Jews Not Welcome", what do they have against us?

When the bell rang, I ran home as fast as I could. There were kids who wanted to beat me up after school.

Filthy Jew!

Things got much worse...

A Jewish youngster has murdered a German diplomat...

Hmm, a perfect excuse to teach all the Jews in Germany a lesson!

We'll "arrange" for the masses to rise up in anger!

On the night of November 9, 1938, gangs of Nazi thugs turned out all over Germany...

There's also a Jewish shop down there!

No, to the synagogue first!

Hit 'em where it hurts!

Our synagogue went up in flames...

Where are the fire trucks?

They're not coming, isn't that obvious?

The clothing store across the street from us was wrecked...

Why isn't anyone stopping this?

They've gone too far now...

This was later called Kristallnacht or the "Night of Broken Glass". Hundreds of synagogues and thousands of shops were destroyed. My uncle was imprisoned in a concentration camp, just like 30,000 other Jews.

We were scared to death. What could we do?

Flee? And where to? So many countries in Europe have closed their borders.

We've booked passage on a ship sailing for Argentina. If I was you, I wouldn't wait much longer.

My father called a colleague in Holland who agreed to help us...

Are you really sure this is a good idea?

Of course! Once Hitler is gone we'll just go home.

Entering the Netherlands wasn't so simple...

You're only welcome here if you have enough money...

I used to have enough, but I had to leave it behind!

Go home then!

But, we were lucky.

Here's our invitation from Professor Bouwer...he's picking us up.

Yes, there's a man waiting for you!

UITGANG
PERRON 1

And that's how we arrived in Amsterdam. With just a few suitcases.

The worst is over, Dr. Hecht. I'm busy arranging a job for you at the hospital where I work...

So what happened finally? Did Esther ever return to Germany?

No, because the war began here...

Hitler continued building a strong and modern army. Newsreel footage of this was shown in the movie theatres...

All people who speak German should live in one country. Germans are superior - the strongest and smartest people in the world.

Without much opposition, Hitler occupied the Rhineland, Austria, Czechoslovakia, making them part of Germany. Then England and France issued an ultimatum: "If Hitler invades Poland, we will declare war on Germany!"

The Netherlands continued to cling to its neutrality...

8

On September 1, 1939, the powerful German Army invaded Poland...

England reacted immediately.

My fellow countrymen... we are at war with Germany...

But nobody helped the Polish Army and they didn't have a chance.

Attack!

This is pointless!

They're too strong.

The radio spoke of atrocities committed against the Poles.

Ready, aim, FIR...

After Poland's defeat, things were quiet for awhile...

Let's hope the worst is over now.

Oh, we needn't worry about anything, after all Holland is neutral...

Yet, I really admire the German army. It's so modern and efficient.

Why don't you just shut up!

In the spring, the German army occupied Norway and Denmark. The Netherlands clung to its neutrality.

The neutrality has gone too far... pretending to defend ourselves against England!

While everybody knows Germany is the real threat!

The Dutch Army was poorly equipped.

Think we can hit anything with this 1896 canon?

I think the rifle I'm using is even a bit older.

We might have had half-a-chance... against the Romans!

On May 10, 1940, I was awakened by the noise of airplanes...

They're going to bomb the Airport! It's a crime!

War, we're at war!

Oh no! What will we do now?

We were all glued to the news!

Shh, the Queen.

People of the Netherlands, last night, without the slightest provocation, the German Army launched a surprise attack on our territory...

EMBAD

CARROSSERIEN

An entire army is falling from the sky!

So much for defending the nation!

Let's hope they all drown in the sea...

The radio reported heavy fighting at the Afsluitdijk, the strategic dam in the North of the country.

Damn! The Dutch are too entrenched!

Their bunkers are too strong!

The Dutch troops put up a brave fight...

They don't call us the elite German forces for nothing. This will be over in no time!

It was such a nerve-racking time... with so much confusion...

The newspaper says the German army has experienced a setback.

It's a bunch of propaganda. We're powerless against the German Army.

It seems thousands are already dead...

The Dutch Queen fled to England.

That's good news because now the Krauts * won't capture her.

What a coward. She's abandoned us.

Non-sense!

* offensive slang for Germans

10

The war reached our doorstep...

Oh my goodness, they're bombing Amsterdam!

They've hit the oil tanks in the harbor!

Now we're doomed...

Esther and her parents tried to flee again...

Why are you leaving?

We're going to try and find a ship that's sailing for England...

But they couldn't... the roads were blocked...

You must go back!

IJmuiden

Amsterdam

Please listen to us, we're Jews... our lives are in danger!

The advance was taking too long for Germany's generals...

We're behind schedule. This battle in the Netherlands has already taken four days!

We'll issue an ultimatum: we'll bomb Rotterdam if they don't capitulate!

While negotiations about the surrender were under way, on May 14, German bombers took off...

This'll be a cinch! Rotterdam doesn't have any anti-aircraft defenses.

The bombers appeared above the center of the city...

What's going on? The ultimatum doesn't expire for three hours!

Heavens... this will be a disaster!

Stay in formation, carpet the city with bombs...open hatch doors...

BOMBS AWAY!!!

That's how the old center of Rotterdam was destroyed...

11

The Germans also threatened to bomb the city of Utrecht...

Countrymen... Today, May 14... the Dutch Army has agreed to lay down its weapons...

15

The next day the German Army rolled into Amsterdam...

Where are we going?

To the Berlage Bridge... it was on the radio.

There's so many of them!

Now, we're in trouble...

The Dutch Nazis were happy about the Occupation...

Welcome to Amsterdam!

Now we're in charge!

We're gonna put things right. Finally!

Look Helena! Your father is directing traffic with that German soldier!

Yes, he's on duty today.

Yesterday, we were fighting them, today we're collaborating...

Much to our surprise, the German soldiers were well-behaved.

Very nice boys, they bought up all my chocolate. Didn't steal a thing, simply paid for it all!

Later...

Huh, there's a hearse in front of our house!

Your mother is crying.

Mother! What's happened?

The old Jewish couple from no. 60... committed suicide!

They were so afraid of the future...

The Occupier immediately disbanded the parliament.

Yes, that was to be expected. Now we really won't have a say.

Wow, this German Army is invincible. Nobody's capable of defeating them!

The newspapers only report what the Germans permit.

...with the defeat of the Netherlands, Belgium and France, the battle now turns to England.

In July 1940

Corrie, I'm a police officer... I can't break the law. I don't want anyone in this house listening to the BBC!!!

You can't be serious?!? How will we get any accurate news about the war? The Krauts only broadcast their lies to us.

Certain items such as coffee, tea, and soap became scarce. People received monthly ration coupons. You needed these coupons to purchase goods.

My mother wants to know if we can get a bit more soap?

No, there's a soap shortage and it's divided as fairly as possible. Your coupon please.

Autumn arrived...

What's wrong Esther?

...sob...at the market-place, Dutch Nazis were fighting with the Jewish merchants!

Don't get so upset. The police will make sure this doesn't happen again.

No, this is exactly how it began in Germany...

My brothers continued fighting with each other...

What discipline! The Dutch can learn a lot from these Germans!

Nonsense, have you forgotten what they're doing in Poland! Wait 'til you really get to know them...

A while later...

How come you know about Poland?

You didn't really think I would obey Father? I listen to the BBC in secret whenever I can...

My father was in a bad mood most of the time. There were lots of changes at the Police Dept.

Believe me Corrie, to advance my career, I have to join the Dutch Nazi Party. Only party members will be promoted.

Have you completely lost your mind?

Once I've signed the Aryan Declaration, then nothing stands in the way...

An Aryan Declaration? I know all about it...

13

The next day they did open fire on the crowd. The strike ended quickly... the streetcars started riding again, each with a policeman aboard.

...all the city employees have gone back to work. I don't need a bullet in my head.

They're still striking in the outskirts of the city... dangerous.

The Germans arrested many protesters.

Has the strike now ended?

Yes, it's pointless for people to resist...

March 1941. For almost a year, the Nazis had tried to convince the Dutch population to join them. However, they had not succeeded.

The Dutch must now choose for National Socialism. You're either with us or against us! We will deal harshly with those who resist!

To prove they meant business, three strikers and fifteen members of a Resistance Group were executed.

C'mon, you're next in line...

Oranje boven

OZO

Still, more and more Dutch people joined the Resistance. For example, illegal newspapers were distributed.

A few classmates and I have an underground school newspaper.

Be careful! You can be arrested for that...

In April, everyone was issued an identity card, a sort of passport.

Take your identity card with you, Corrie!

Ration coupons, identity cards... what will they think up next?!

But we were doing a lot better than Esther and her parents...

What's with your father? He didn't even say hello!

He isn't allowed to work at the hospital anymore. Jewish doctors are only allowed to treat Jewish patients.

Jews were isolated step-by-step. One warm day, we wanted to go to the swimming pool...

No Jews Allowed?!

Then I won't go swimming either!

VERBODEN VOOR JODEN

ZWEMBAD

15

My family was always arguing.

Now, you listen to me young man...

1 9

...the *spertijd** also applies to you. You'd better be home on time tonight!

Just because you play policeman out there, doesn't mean you get to be one here too!

* *curfew requiring people to leave the streets and be home at a prescribed hour*

All your rules make me insane...

Things were bad at home.

This is the last time I'm going to warn you, boy!

I'll do what I want!

...to preserve Western Civilization... we're fighting the barbarians from the East...

Father! Theo! Hitler has attacked Russia!

...we are faithful to our leader Adolf Hitler...

...from Finland to the Black Sea, the German Army is advancing, supported by Finnish, Italian, Romanian and Hungarian comrades.

The following day the papers were filled with news.

Russia is a goner!

23 juni 1941

Proclamatie van Hitler aan Duitsche volk

Rusland

Groot-Duitsche Rijk

Gevechten aan de geheele Russische grens gisteren begonnen.

Wat doet Nederland?

ACTIE IN HET OOSTEN WORDT STELSELMATIG VOORTGEZET

I'm going to Esther's...

What a great adventure!

I feel much more at home at their house.

16

Hi, Mrs. Hecht. Is Esther around?

Come in. Esther has gotten some bad news...

I can't go back to school after the summer. Jewish students have to go to separate schools.

That's terrible!

We can't do anything about it... But the new school is close to our school...

At least we'll still be able to walk to school together!

It was more enjoyable to be at Esther's, but her family also had their worries.

I already said it in 1938! We should have gone to America.

How could we have known the Nazis would occupy the Netherlands?

I'm so glad we can go back to school...

Me too, I get crazy at home...

V = Victorie
Duitschland wint op alle fronten

I'll see you right after school!

My history teacher at school was replaced by a member of the Dutch Nazi Party. We immediately hated him.

...and in this book, Hitler explained his ideas. He already wrote in 1925 that...

De strijd tegen het communisme is een strijd om te overleven

Leningrad

Moskou

Krim

Why is Esther so late?

Esther! What happened?

VERORDENING

...there were boys waiting for us after school...they called us names and hurled a stone through a window of our school...

Cowards!

Perhaps my father can do something about this...

How can you enforce all these German regulations?

We have to. They're in charge.

I have no time to talk about this... duty calls.

Father! You have to help Esther!

Help? What's wrong?

Esther and her classmates are being harassed by some bullies. Isn't there something you can do?

Don't blow this all out of proportion...

Helena, Jews shouldn't expect any protection from the police. I don't understand why Father is still a policeman...

What other choices does he have? Resigning? How would we get by?

Just a few weeks later, a letter arrived from Theo:

... I'm now at basic training...

Men, you will soon become part of the brotherhood defending the Greater German Reich...

20

... it is very hard, but we're learning a lot...

I want to hear those boots, you bunch of weaklings! We're going to make you real soldiers!

... and my closet has never been so orderly...

Your closet is a mess! Take your neighbor as an example. Your leave is cancelled!

... and if we go to the fairgrounds, I'll never look foolish again.

Very good shot! That's what we need!

... We're also taught about Adolf Hitler's ideology.

Our greatest enemies are the Jews and the Russians. It is a battle about life or death!

STRIJDT MEE !

...Taking the oath of allegiance was a very solemn moment...

We swear our loyalty to Adolf Hitler, Führer of the Greater German Reich.

Then a note arrived that Theo was being sent to the front...

Oh how awful! We'll probably never see him again!

Stop sniveling. He'll be fine!

KOFFIE SURROGAAT

Gébé EI-SURROGAAT

ébé rogaat voor CACAO

A month later, another letter arrived from Theo:

I'm now at the front...

Where are they getting all these Russian soldiers? Everyone said Russia was almost defeated!

Yeah, almost...

While the combat in Russia dragged on, in December 1941, Japan launched a surprise attack on the American fleet at Pearl Harbor...

And now what?!

Japan was an ally of Hitler's Germany.

...and that's why our Führer Adolf Hitler has now declared war on the United States...

Now the whole world is at war!

...our trusted ally Japan will drive the Americans, British, and the Dutch out of Asia...

Oh, terrible! I hope nothing bad happens to Aunt Riek...

Aunt Riek was my mother's sister. In 1935, she went to live in the Dutch East Indies. Now it's called Indonesia...

Is that great dagger from there?

Yes, it's called a Javanese kris.

My Aunt Riek lived on Java, one of the islands in the Dutch East Indies. I always dreamed about visiting her.

Nederlandsch Oost-Indië vergeleken met Europa

Schoolplaat XIV

If you compare the size of our colony to Europe...

21

Japan had been preparing for this war for years.

We want to rule Asia the same way that Germany rules Europe.

Asia for the Asians! Westerners, Go Home!

After the attack on Pearl Harbor, Japan invaded the Dutch East Indies, Malaysia, and the Philippines... and they weren't finished...

We have an immense task before us...

22

A naval fleet of American, British, and Dutch ships went down fighting...

The enemy has been defeated...

Tomorrow, we will take the island of Java!

Many natives of the Dutch East Indies hoped Japan would free them from Dutch dominance.

TOKO MAKASSAR

MODE

The Japanese will help us gain independence!

I'm afraid they're going to be our new oppressor...

Aunt Riek was there when the Japanese Army landed...

Belandas * Go Home!

What will happen now?

*The Dutch

Many Europeans were imprisoned in Japanese camps. Also Aunt Riek, Uncle Cor, and their son André.

You have 15 minutes to pack what you can carry. You're going to a camp and your property will be confiscated!

After the war, we finally heard what had happened to them. They went through terrible times...

Gran, that dagger, uh... the kris...

It's yours, if you want it...

...but during that time, I didn't think about the Dutch East Indies much!

Discrimination against Jews increased...

There are so many restrictions...

...no biking, driving, going to the zoo, we're not allowed in the library...

...we may no longer belong to a sports club...

We're not even allowed to sit in this small park anymore... everything's forbidden!

Voor Joden verboden

Wim joined the Resistance...

I'll distribute them this week...

Be careful, all right?

Printing and distributing underground newspapers was punishable by death.

Father mustn't find out...

HET PAROOL
APRIL 1942
VRIJ ONVERVEERD

I secretly passed copies to our neighbors.

There's an article on doctors and the Resistance.

VERDUISTERD
BESCHERMD

Hi, may I come in? What's wrong?

Esther really needs you now...

Esther!

Oh no, huh, what's the meaning of this?

Those bastards! Now they can easily see who's Jewish. It's so degrading!

I couldn't do anything to help... Jews even had to pay for the stars themselves! This is the one Esther gave me...

24

What if you just didn't sew it on your clothes?

Jood

The punishment was severe. You also always had to have your identity card with you. This was mine, but there was a capital J on the identity cards of Jews!

It was spring and beautiful weather, but things at home were bad.

What were you thinking... bringing these underground newspapers here?!

Don't do that! I have to distribute those papers!

You will not! It's forbidden and now it's over! Say goodbye to this junk!

You will stop this immediately! You're putting our lives at risk!

I won't stop... it's much too important.

When father was out, we listened to Radio Orange, the Dutch station broadcasting from London.

...so be it then, we'll get the latest news this way!

This is Radio Orange, the voice of fighting Holland...

...the Germans have not managed to reconquer the area around Moscow.

Yes! For the first time the German army has been stopped!

But what about Theo?

A few weeks later we heard from Theo.

I was wounded during a bombardment, but was very lucky. I'm up for some leave soon and I'll come home to recover...

We went to visit him in the hospital.

25

I'm so happy to see you. I'm already feeling much better.

We fought hard against the Russians, but the winter was unbearable.

We don't even have decent winter jackets.

The Russians are used to this dreadful cold!

We thought it'd be an easy victory but the Russian Army was very determined...

Luckily, the winter is almost over...

We were attacked at the beginning of April...

TAKE COVER!!! AIR RAID!

AAH!!

26

My friend Karel is dead. Many comrades gave up their lives for the cause. Yet, sometimes I really wonder...

What?

Awful things happen in wartime...

One day we were in a village behind the front lines...

What kind of soldiers are those? Never seen them on the front!

Where are they taking those civilians?

Those army units carry out special missions.

Civilians? Those are Jews, man.

Special missions? What kind of special mis...

RATATATATATATATAT

...sions?

It can't be true!

I don't want you to go back, Theo!

But I have to! We must win this war...

You'll be careful, my boy?

Say hello to Father...

That was the last time I saw Theo. One afternoon a letter arrived...

Mother! What's wrong?

...killed in action for Führer, Folk and Fatherland...

My mother was terribly upset... but my father scarcely reacted...

My mother tried talking to him about it.

Are you listening to me?!?

Not another word about Theo!

My parents argued a great deal.

I'm not blind. Don't you think I see how the police collaborate with the Germans...

You'll have dirty hands!

What do you want? That I resign, be sent off to Germany?

Maybe that would be better...

What nonsense!

You going out? Let me come? They're driving me crazy!

No, you can't come.

Then I'll go out alone!

Why are you outside? It's going to rain!

Much better than being inside!

27

In the weeks following, more and more Jews received a call up...

You must report, what choice is there?

Just don't go...

But then the police come to get you...

29

Many Jews who chose to ignore the call-up were rounded up.

Handy that we know exactly where the Jews live...

Outside... right now!

We can't go yet, our daughter is still at school...

We'll also go pick her up...

The Nazis organized razzias. They would close off a street or a neighborhood and search all the houses. One day there was a razzia nearby my school.

All Jews must leave their homes right now. Bring only one suitcase along with you!

Your identity card...

Teachers from Esther's school were rounded up too...

Mr. De Winter will not be returning. French class is now cancelled...

§12 → 5 t/m 12

J'habite un
Dans la ma

Her classmates disappeared without warning...

Martin and Tineke are gone...

Let's hope they went into hiding...

It's difficult to go into hiding... You need money and the help of non-Jewish friends...

And it's dangerous, because if you're caught...

We're going to try anyway...

There were more and more razzias in Amsterdam. Many Jews were rounded up and registered...

...they were then taken by streetcar to the train station.

Last year the conductors went out on strike...

Now they're simply too afraid to help us...

I'm happy we're not Jews.

Afterwards, they were sent to Westerbork Transit Camp.

Anyone who disobeys our rules, will immediately be transported to the East!

Trains left weekly from Westerbork carrying men, women, and children to unknown destinations in Eastern Europe.

I hope we'll be reunited with our parents...

Be quiet! Hurry up!

They treat us like we're cattle...

We'll probably be picked up soon as well.

Can't you go somewhere?

BEPERKTE BEWEGINGSVRIJHEID VOOR JODEN

Possibly...my father is trying to arrange a hiding place for us.

Esther and her parents were running out of time...

When are you all going into hiding?

It's almost arranged...

Here, this necklace is for you. As a token of our close friendship. This might be the last time we see each other...

They were too late. One morning in September 1942...

Having to do this in your own neighborhood...

I hear you. I couldn't get reassigned...

Jews live up there on the third floor. Make sure nobody escapes.

Family Meijer! Downstairs right now!

My mother was shocked when she saw that my father had been assigned to that razzia...

Oh no! He said only Dutch Nazis working for the police did these round ups.

Waaah... Mommy!

Keep moving!

But... wait, that's... our neighbor!

Can't you please help us?

31

...Esther... she's still at school. Please warn and tell her where they're taking us...

Uh... I don't... I'll see what I can do...

Faster! Faster!

I'm... wait... OU!

Uh.. um, uh, easy on these people. They're not resisting...

I'll wait here for Esther. Then you can travel together!

When the razzia was over, my father lingered behind.

Too many Jewish children get away...

I'll pick her up and then report in...

It's best if I wait here for Esther to return...

I saw you going into the neighbors house. What's going on?

I promised that I would bring Esther to join her parents...

Father! How can you help the Germans?

If I didn't, they'd just fire me on the spot! Don't think I'm happy about this, but...

Now, you've gone too far!

Just shut up! I've heard enough. I'm going to get Esther!

It was late when my father got home. I had stayed up until he returned.

There he is! Alone!

Father, what happened? Where's Esther?

32

I did what I had to do. Discussion closed!

What my father did then... I never forgave him for it. Look, this is the necklace that Esther gave me. I wear it all the time.

My life was changed forever. I missed my best friend so much. Everything I saw around me, reminded me of her...

Oh, they're emptying out more Jewish homes.

Like the upstair's neighbors... Oh Esther...

What do you do with all these things?

Goes to people in Germany who've been hit by the Allied bombings.

I can't stand being at home, Wim. Can't I help you with the newspaper runs?

It's too dangerous...

I know, but I still want to do it...

I'll talk to my friends about it. It's true, a girl attracts less attention...

There's something I have to do. Go straight home.

33

We all have our secrets. Wim in the Resistance... Father and his work...

We had less and less contact with Father.

You use this house like it's a hotel...

Fine! Go hide at work! I'm surprised you're not working more overtime.

Grumble...

The weeks passed...

I'm going to get some air. I still have ration coupons for meat. Maybe there is some... You'll stay here?

Sigh... yes, mother.

Later...

Hey sis. Is the old man still at work?

Yes, and mom's asleep. She waited in line for hours.

Your attention for an extra bulletin from the headquarters of the Führer...

...in Russia... heroic until the last man and bullet, the German Sixth Army has been defeated at Stalingrad.

Did you hear that?

The German Army's been hit hard!

BRRRRrrrrrrrooooaaaa

Listen! British planes...

I'll turn off the lights, so we can see! Pull back the blackout curtains!

...a period of mourning has been declared in the entire Reich, but...

They're headed for Germany!

Germany is being attacked from all sides. The war is almost over...

We read in the newspapers that German cities were bombed. But many Allied planes were shot down en route to Germany.

I've lost control! We're going down!

Where are we?

I'm not really sure!

34

Some pilots managed to parachute from their planes in time. The Resistance found them a hiding place quite often...

Speak up! Any sign of the crew?

I saw somebody on the road...

Don't know...

Via Radio Orange broadcasts, we heard that the German Army in Russia had to carry on retreating...

So, it was sink or swim for them...

Exactly! In Berlin, Minister of Propaganda Goebbels, incited the German people to fight to the bitter end.

The English say that you're tired of the war... that's why I'm asking you...

...DO YOU WANT TOTAL WAR?!?

TOTALER KRIEG - KÜRZESTER KRIEG

YESSSSS!!!

Many German men were called up for the army. The Dutch military, captured in May 1940 and later released, were ordered to go work in Germany. People really resented this.

Naturally, our soldiers don't want to go to Germany to work. This calls for a strike!

Is striking a good idea?

NEDERLANDERS STAAKT!
ALGEMENE STAKIN...

At the end of April 1943, strikes began all over Holland...

BEKENDMAKING

Demonstrators will be shot...

The first protesters were executed right away...

That should scare them off...

Nobody will dare strike now!

The strike was over within a matter of days...

It's an uneven fight...

That won't stop us...

Resistance increased...

What's happening here is a disgrace!

We can't just sit here!

You're right!

There was an armed resistance...

Deserved it! Now, he can't betray anymore Resistance people!

Let's go!

There was sabotage...

So, now the Krauts can use carrier pigeons...

Resistance groups became much better organized.

We're preparing a vital operation. Can you help us get some German Army uniforms?

We need ten false identity cards...

Not only Jews, but Resistance fighters also had to go into hiding. The LO was a nationwide network that helped these people by arranging hiding places for them...

You're already the fifth this week...

Our Resistance group was betrayed.

When Wim turned 18, he received a call-up...

I have to go work in Germany!

You're not going to do that?!

I'll go into hiding tomorrow. You tell Mother?

Of course!

1943

I'll miss him so...

The LO arranged for Wim to hide at a farm in the East of the Netherlands.

You're not our only guest...

Thanks! If I can ever help you in return?

Welcome, son. You'll have to share the hayloft with a few other people...

No problem!

Wim was given false papers and worked with the local Resistance...

Wim de Jong...Hmm.

36

His first missions were simple. Take money and ration coupons to people in hiding.

Gasp, gasp... there's not much chance of running into the Germans on such a miserable day...

...later dangerous. Weapon drops...

Hurry! I hear a car coming. Let's go!

Good, precisely as planned...

...the robbery of a distribution center...

If you just stay calm, you'll be fine!

Enough ration coupons for hundreds in hiding.

The Nazis crushed the Resistance using any means...

Quite a good catch today!

We tortured that prisoner until he told us their names...

Many members of the Resistance were executed by the Nazis...

Long live the Queen!

FIRE!

May you burn in Hell!

There were also those Dutch who helped the Germans, and made lots of money...

They want more bunkers from us, in case of an invasion...

Fine! We'll be rich!

Others profited from the shortages. Black marketeers.

Cigarettes and Dutch gin... 400 guilders *

You're a profiteer!

Let's buy the stuff anyway...

* Today around $250

37

And always that threat of being secretly betrayed by someone who was a snitch.

...there are people hiding at no. 8 Kerkstraat...

Most of the Dutch just tried to go about their normal lives...

HET VERLEDEN
GRANDIOSE SUCCESFILM met ZARAH LEANDER

ZARAH LEANDER   HANS STÖWE

Luckily, we can still go to the movies!

To forget the war for a moment...

Many thought about their own needs first...

The man from no. 15 was arrested!

His own fault.

It's best to just mind your own business...

BAKKER

I was so lonesome during the winter of 1943-1944...

Esther gone, delivered to the Germans by my own father... my brothers gone...

I hardly saw my father. He usually worked the nightshift to avoid quarrelling with my mother...

Helena, please go see if the grocery store has kerosene for the lamp. Shut the door quietly...

Sigh! Yes, Mother... I know, Father is sleeping.

38

I just hope there isn't a long line...

There she is!

That was quick! Mother will be happy with the kerosene.

KRUIDENIE

WINTERHULP wu geven 5% van onze winst

It feels as if I'm being followed!

Not now! A razzia!

Run, it's the Krauts!

RIVOLI

ufa Film

MARIKA RÖKK

KASSA

Awful! To have to go to Germany...

Pick up all the men between 18 and 50!

Forced labor...

PTT

Where did that guy go?

Helena van Dort?

OH!

?!?

Sorry, I didn't mean to scare you. Wim sent me...

Wim... my brother Wim? I... how is...?

He's doing just fine and said I could ask you to help us...

Help? How can I help?

39

We need somebody who's prepared to act as a courier. It's important and your brother said...

...that I would help out... It's true!

I distributed underground newspapers that were printed in a basement.

Keep going with that stinking fish!

VISHANDEL KOLK

Pfff... that was a close call... If he only had a clue...

My father handed over our radio when he had to. My new friends had cleverly hidden their radio...

Umph!... Let's see what Radio Orange has to report!

They should really make smaller radios...

People of Western Europe, a landing was made this morning on the coast of France...

The invasion! Finally!

1944
6
juni

That was a memorable summer. The good news kept coming... Paris was liberated at the end of August.

...together with our Russian allies, we're going to liberate Europe...

Paris has been liberated! Hitler's order to destroy the city was ignored by the German general in command there.

And then, on September 4, 1944...

Helena! Hurry! You won't believe your ears.

4

Radio Orange reporting. The Allied Forces have crossed into the Netherlands.

Unbelievable! It's going so well...

Finally! The Liberation...

The next day, the wildest rumors were flying ...

The Brits have crossed our southern border!

Americans have been sighted close by! We have to hurry to the city line! Our liberators will soon be in Amsterdam!

Where are they all going?

To Germany! The rats are deserting the sinking ship!

Look! There's those Nazi collaborators! *

* people who helped the German Occupier

We got excited too soon. The rumors weren't true. That day was later called "Dolle Dinsdag" (Crazy Tuesday). However, the South of the Netherlands was liberated.

We'll cross the Rhine at Arnhem...

Once we've crossed over, Holland will be liberated and then we'll advance into Germany...

A huge Allied assault of the most important bridges by Arnhem and Nijmegen took place on September 17, 1944...

Hello, I'm Wim de Jong. I'm carrying vital information from the Resistance.

Jolly good, old boy. Why is the German opposition here so strong?

An SS Armored Division...

All right. Contact HQ* for further instructions.

* Headquarters

The assault failed...

We have to retreat. Join us if you like...

Eh... yes... sure!

The Dutch government exiled in London called for a railway strike to hinder the Occupier, so hardly any food could be delivered by train...

Life is going to get even worse...

Alles nu op de bon

Yes, now we have to stand in line for everything!

I'm afraid these rations are even less than we had before...

I'm so hungry!

The winter of 1944-1945 became known as the Hunger Winter.

Quickly! Hide the bread under your coat.

Hurry! The Germans are coming!

Give it... umph!

I can hear their dogs barking.

BAKKERIJ

HALT! STEHEN BLEIBEN!!

What do you have there, boy?!

𝔚𝔬𝔬𝔣! 𝔚𝔬𝔬𝔣! 𝔚𝔬𝔬𝔣!

There were many razzias. Fifty thousand men and boys were transported from Rotterdam. They were put to work shoring up the German line of defense.

I don't care if each and everyone of you drops dead digging. As long as I get my anti-tank ditch!

Coal was scarce...

Luckily we still have that old wood stove. It's good for burning everything.

Now if we just had something to cook on it... what a shame...

Wood for burning was gathered up from everywhere. Empty houses were stripped...

Take care! A house like that collapsed!

Hey, what would the people who lived here think of this mess?

They were Jews...

Mother stop, otherwise the sack will be too heavy.

But that wood from in-between the rails burns so well!

One morning in January 1945...

Mother! I've been asked to take a group of children to Friesland. If they stay here they'll starve, but farmers there still have some food.

Gulp...

I hoped that I could just stay there...

Will you write?

I hope they'll be okay...

Oh, the Red Cross... they're not a target!

41

4

Soup kitchens where people could get something to eat opened in the West of the country.

What is this anyway? It looks like glue!

It's stew.

Look how hungry they are...

Poor things...

My mother decided to go to the countryside with a neighbor to try and find some food.

We can put a lot in this baby carriage.

I hope they still have some food left for us...

My mother and her neighbor were not the only ones who set off on such a journey...

I'm afraid that some people will never make it home...

What choice do they have? Dying of starvation?

Can't you give me some more potatoes for this necklace? It's a family heirloom.

No, then we don't have any for ourselves.

The journeys were hard... the disappointments many.

We're almost hom... oh no!

The Landwacht! *

* Auxiliary police comprised of Dutch Nazis

At least we didn't confiscate everything...

Bastards!

More than 20,000 people died of hunger and cold that winter... When we were utterly desperate, food fell from the sky...

That British plane is coming in very low...

The Germans are allowing it. Their anti-aircraft gunners won't shoot them down...

The food shortages in Friesland weren't so bad, but we were still happy when the spring of 1945 arrived...

Thanks for letting me stay until the Liberation...

It won't be long now...

I just heard the latest news report...

Hitler is now completely surrounded by the Allies...

!!!

Once the Brits and Americans advance from the West and join the Russians from the East, the war will be over...

SCHOOL PLAAT 1928

Berlijn

Hitler is trapped...

43

Friesland was liberated on April 15, 1945...

Now it is really almost over! The Germans are withdrawing!

...on May 5, 1945 we finally heard the news that we had been waiting for...

The German Army has surrendered...

We're finally free!

The war is over!

In the middle of the festivities, my Frisian father arrived with bad news.

?!?

Helena! Something's happened in Amsterdam.

Yesterday, German soldiers opened fire on the crowd celebrating downtown. Many people were killed or wounded...

Fire! That'll teach them to celebrate!

RATATATATA

Perhaps my mother has been hurt... or my father...

I need to go to Amsterdam!

Of course!

The next day...

You can hitch a ride on this BS*truck all the way to Alkmaar.

Thanks for everything!

I want to go home too!

You have to stay a bit longer...

* Dutch National Reserve

4

Upon arriving in Alkmaar...

Come dance with me, girl!

Uh, no, but thanks...

I'll dance again when I know my mother is okay...

NOOO!!! Leave me alone!

Should have thought of that sooner!

What's going on over there?!

Sit still, before I cut off your ear!

Where's your Kraut boyfriend now?!

Sob...

NSB RAT verrajer

KRAUT WHORE! KRAUT WHORE!

How awful...

I wanted to get going and I had some luck...

Need a lift some-where, doll face?!

Eh, ja... Yes!

So... tomorrow I can hitch a ride with you to Amsterdam?

Only if you come to our party tonight!

Sigh, all right then!

44

Come with me baby. I've got chocolate and nylons just for you!

I'm not for sale!

THANK YOU BOYS

Yu haf zikarets vor my?

Finally, I was back in Amsterdam.

Hey girl, can I drop you off somewhere?

Look! They've made a floating bridge from all the ferries.

My heart was pounding as we rode into my street...

Bedankt....uh, thanks. For taking me right to my door!

Courtesy of the Army!

Thanks boys!

Sigh... aah, to be young again!

45

Gulp... I hope everything is okay...

What a mess! This is not like my mother...

I thought I heard something. I'm so glad you're back, Helena!

Hello! Is everything okay? Have you seen my mother?

She's staying with your Aunt Bep and is fine, but your father...

I must go to her right away!

Oh, the neighbor wanted to tell me about my father...

...I wonder what's happened to him?

Those who collaborated should be dealt with!

Yes, they should be severely punished!

Gulp...

Luckily, Aunt Bep and my mother were at home...

Oh, my dear child. I'm so glad that you're back!

Oh Mother, it's so good to see you too! But... what's happened to Father, where is he?!

Oh Helena! They came and got Father...

The BS arrested everyone they suspected of collaborating with the Germans...

Let's go, you traitor!

You're mistaken!

We'll see about that later!

They have locked them up in the storehouses in the harbor. It's so terrible!

Don't you dare complain. Because otherwise...

VERBODEN

How humiliating...

A week later...

Hello Aunt Bep! Are Mother and Helena here?

Of course! Come right on in!

Helena!

Oh, Wim!

Oh my boy, I have been so worried!

46

I enlisted with an English Army unit. I also met up with the Russian fighting troops...

Hey, English! You drink wodka?!

I'm from Holland! Got any ol' Dutch gin?

...the Russians told us the most awful stories. They liberated camps in Poland that the Nazis built especially to kill as many people as possible... and in particular the Jews of Europe...

So they were murdered with this gas?

They thought they were going to shower and...

Did the Nazis tattoo numbers on your arms?

Yes, on the arms of all the people who could work. Children and the elderly were killed when they arrived...

Most prisoners died from exhaustion or were murdered in the gas chambers. Also thousands of Jews from the Netherlands.

Oh Esther! She must be dead.

Good gracious!

The survivors of the camps began returning. For a while, I went to the Central Train Station everyday...

Did you know an Esther Hecht?

No.

Sob... it's hopeless... nobody's seen her...

Some more very sad news arrived...

This letter was just delivered...

What is it mother?

...due to an unfortunate accident, your husband has died in prison.

A week later I was standing beside my father's grave...

Oh, why did he collaborate with the Germans?

The war in Asia didn't end until August 15, 1945. Japan surrendered after two atom bombs were dropped on Hiroshima and Nagasaki. We were very worried about Aunt Riek...

It's a letter from Uncle Cor...

Please read it aloud, Mother!

Terrible things were done to them...

Europeans were imprisoned in camps. And the men were separated from the women and children.

Cor thought he would never see Riek and André again...

Farewell, Riek!

I love you Cor!

Papa!

The prisoners in the camp had to pay their daily respects to the Japanese Emperor Hirohito.

Bow, lower, lower...!

The camp guards handed out cruel punishments.

15 lashes is enough...

That'll teach them!

Pens and writing paper are forbidden...

47

When boys turned 12, they were transferred to the men's camp...

Be brave, son!

Sob... Will I ever see him again?

The men were often forced to carry out heavy labor...

I can't handle this anymore, Cor...

急いで！ *)

C'mon!

*Hurry up!

Many prisoners died of disease and malnutrition.

Give this to my wife...

Of course...

Some no longer believed they would survive. Still, others tried to keep everybody's spirits up...

...the Japanese are going to lose the war...

...it won't be long now...

I wonder how Riek and André are?

Uncle Cor described the Liberation.

Look! It's American! The first one in three years!

Unbelievable!

One morning, at the end of August...

What's happened?

Where did all the Japs go?

Major De Wildt wants to speak...

The Japanese Emperor has decided to stop fighting... we're free!

They have lost the war!

Now everything will return to normal...

They were celebrating outside the camp as well... but it would never be the way it was before the war.

MERDEKA! * We're not your colony anymore!

We are now a Free Republic.

What kind of non-sense is this?

*Freedom

I just want to go back to my plantation...

48

This plantation is now ours!

Let's go, before they kill us!

The camp was the safest place...

We'll be okay here.

Of course we will, the Japanese have orders from the English to protect us...

MERDEKA!

But some of the Japanese gave weapons to the rebellious Indonesians.

Yes! This will come in very handy!

Now we're in control!

A British Army battalion finally reached the camp where Riek and Cor had been reunited...

...I'm handing over this camp to you...

Listen... your men have orders to protect the people in this camp.

49

The Dutch living here must be taken to a safe area of the island.

Hai!

That's how the Japanese ended up helping the English...

This route is too dangerous. The rebels have rifles and even machine guns!

Gulp... is that so?

An ambush!

Aaah, Mother... I've been hit!

Not all the liberated prisoners reached the coast safely.

Oh no! Riek! Don't leave me!

Survived three years in a camp to die anyway...

...sob... my only sister...

Oh, I'm so sorry Mother... but luckily you still have us!

We did not know what to do next...

How will we go on?

In the spring of 1946 my mother came to a decision.

So many horrible things have happened here...

I want to go back to my hometown...

Sounds like a good plan!

Count me in...

A month later the moving truck was on our doorstep.

It's better that they're leaving...

Everbody here knows her husband collaborated with the Germans.

He even took part in razzias in his own neighborhood!

50

I hope we can now put the war behind us, Helena.

I wonder...

What should we do with father's uniform?

Dear me, such devastation!

...but look how hard their working!

Hello, I'm your neighbor from no. 47. Do you need a hand?

She's a war widow from the big city.

Yes, all those poor victims of the hunger winter.

So they never found out that your father...

...had helped the Germans? No! Thank goodness.

So then what happened? Did your mother remarry? And what happened to Wim?

My mother never really recovered from the war. She died in 1954...

Things would have been different without that rotten war...

Perhaps, but we'll never know...

Then a few years after the war ended, I met your grandfather...

Uh... Helena, uh... would you like to dance?

Hee hee... I thought you'd never ask, Kees.

Rock Around

We married soon after. It was the time of the post-war reconstruction and we didn't have much money.

Go easy on the rice! During the war it was worth a fortune!

To the happy couple!!!

Wim emigrated to Canada...

I hope he'll write.

Oh, now I'm all alone!

You have me, sweetheart!

We lived in my mother's house for a short while, but...

If our house is ready on time, then the little one will be born there.

Your father was born there in 1962, Jeroen...

I miss my family... and Esther...

I often thought about Esther... especially each year on Memorial Day, May 4.

Now, two minutes of silence to remember the victims of the war...

1940 1945

Look at the time! You'd better hurry home, Jeroen. Or your mother will be angry with me!

Call and say I'm on my way...

Your kris...

...now I'm going to hear it!

Why are you so late, Jeroen?!

Sorry! Grandma was telling me about the war.

Yes, he just walked in...

Every year she dragged me to the ceremony to commemorate the dead. So I'd watch out!

But, she never talks about the war...

And what about that stuff to sell on Queen's Day?

I completely forgot... She let me have this dagger, but I won't sell it! Tomorrow, I'll go by her house again.

Fantastic, that I finally found all these back issues of my favorite fishing magazine...

On May 4...

Gran didn't sound good on the phone...

Grandma, mom lent me your key! Is everything okay with you?

Oh, sweet boy! I sprained my ankle and can't walk at all!

Now I can't go to the memorial service.

52

I'll go for you!

Gasp... I hope I'm not too late...

53

I've lived in the United States for more than fifty years. But during the war I was hidden in a village nearby...

Phew... just in time...

I survived the persecution of the Jews...

My friend Helena, who wasn't Jewish, was a great comfort to me.

Huh?

Thank you, Mrs. Leibowitz, for that moving story! And now for the traditional two minutes of silence...

Impossible! But...

Could it be?

Mind if I ask you something?

Of course not...

Is Leibowitz your married name?

Yes, but my maiden name used to be Hecht, Esther Hecht.

!!!

Really!... You have... with me... please come with me. It's not far.

If it's so important...

A bit later...

I have the key, because my grandma sprained her ankle.

That's a shame, but I don't understand...

Look, someone you haven't seen in a long time...

?!?

Esther?

Helena?

Esther! How is it possible...

To see you again... It's a miracle!

I spent two years in hiding. First around here and later with a couple who lived further South...

We were liberated in September 1944.

This isn't really our niece, but Esther, a Jewish girl...

I thought so all along, but sometimes it's better to play dumb.

54

There were lots of festivities, but I kept thinking about my parents...

Hurrah!

Hurrah! Long live the Queen!

Where could they be?

After the rest of the Netherlands was liberated, I returned to Amsterdam...

Sorry about the bumpy ride...

As long as I get there...

I went to my house but my parents weren't there. Nobody was at your house either. I didn't know where you all were...

I can't help you, haven't seen them...

You sure?

I only moved in recently...

Shortly afterwards, I heard that my parents had been murdered in Auschwitz. Nobody from my family in Germany survived the war either... I was all alone...

I had a chance to go to the United States...

If only we had kept going after Kristallnacht in Germany...

I married Harry Leibowitz. He also had no family anymore...

Mazel tov!

JUST MARRIED

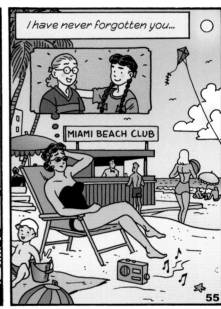

I have never forgotten you...

MIAMI BEACH CLUB

55

Some time ago I received an invitation to speak on Dutch Memorial Day... and now I've found you again...

I always thought you had died... that you were murdered in a horrible concentration camp.

Didn't your father ever tell you what happened?

What?

When I came home from school that day, your father was waiting for me...

Hello, what's wrong?

Just come with me!

He wanted to help me!

I have strict orders to deliver this Jewess where she belongs!

Yes sir!

I gave him the address of a dear friend of my parents and he took me there immediately.

I will say that I couldn't find her after school.

Esther! Come inside quickly!

56

What! Did my father save you? It's amazing!

Oh Esther, we have so much to catch up on...

Uh oh, I'm outta here, once is enough...

Bye... I gotta be home on time!

POK

Drawings
Eric Heuvel

Scenario
Eric Heuvel
Menno Metselaar (Anne Frank House)
Ruud van der Rol (Anne Frank House)
Hans Groeneweg (Resistance Museum Friesland)

English Translation
Lorraine T. Miller (Epicycles, Amsterdam)

Creative Process Support
Ruud de Grefte

Coloring
Hanneke Bons

Typesetting
Rudy Vrooman

Research and Documentation
Jacqueline Koerts

Design
Karel Oosting, Amsterdam

Production
Anne Frank House, Amsterdam

A FAMILY SECRET was originally published in Dutch
as DE ONTDEKKING, thanks in part to funding provided
by the Ministry of Public Health, Welfare and Sport (VWS)
in the Netherlands.

We are thankful to the many people who offered their commentary and advice in the planning and creation of this comic book:

Liesbeth van der Horst (Dutch Resistance Museum, Amsterdam)

Hetty Berg (Stichting Het Indisch Huis, The Hague)

Annemiek Gringold and Petra Katzenstein (Jewish Historical Museum, Amsterdam)

Dirk Mulder (Memorial Center Camp Westerbork)

Nine Nooter (National Committee May 4th and 5th)

Erik Somers (Netherlands Institute for War Documentation / NIOD)

Stef Temming (National War and Resistance Museum, Overloon)

Christel Tijenk (National Monument Camp Vught)

Truus Vélu (Resistance Museum Zuid-Holland, Gouda)

Jan-Durk Tuinier and Geu Visser (Memorial Center Fort de Bilt, Utrecht)

Mieke Sobering (Anne Frank House)

Tom van der Geugten (Fontys Secondary Teacher Training College, Tilburg)

VMBO (Vocational High School) Teachers (and students)

Wim Borghuis and Hans Werker (CSG De Goudse Waarden, Gouda)

Henk Botter (Wellantcollege, Alphen aan den Rijn)

Anke van den Tempel (Montessori College Oost, Amsterdam)

Adult Education Teachers

Chris van Asperen (ROC Rijn IJssel College Arnhem)

Merel Borgesius (ROC of Amsterdam)

Primary School Teachers

Sijmen Sijtsma and Lolkje Algra (Prof. Grewelschool, Leeuwarden)

Matty Delgrosso (OBS Grou, Grou)

Daniëlle Dijkmeijer (Prins Constantijnschool PCBO, Leeuwarden)

Jan Veltman and Jeanne Minks (Albertine Agnesschool PCBO, Leeuwarden)